T0354009

Wonderful WORLD

SECOND EDITION

GRAMMAR BOOK

Australia · Brazil · Mexico · Singapore · United Kingdom · United States

Contents

			Page
Unit 1			
Lesson 1	A/an		4
Lesson 2	Personal pronouns		6
	To be (affirmative)		7
Lesson 3	To be (affirmative)		8
Unit 2			
Lesson 1	Plurals		10
Lesson 2	To be (negative)		12
Lesson 3	To be (questions and short answers)		14
Review: Units 1 – 2			16
Unit 3			
Lesson 1	This/that		18
Lesson 2	These/those		20
Lesson 3	What's this/that? What are these/those?		22
Unit 4			
Lesson 1	There is … / There are … (affirmative)		24
Lesson 2	There is … / There are … (negative, questions and short answers)		26
Lesson 3	A, an, the		28
Review: Units 3 – 4			30
Unit 5			
Lesson 1	Have got (affirmative)		32
Lesson 2	Have got (negative)		34
Lesson 3	Have got (questions and short answers)		36
Unit 6			
Lesson 1	Possessive adjectives		38
Lesson 2	Possessive 's		40
Lesson 3	Order of adjectives		42
Review: Units 5 – 6			44

Contents

			Page
Unit 7			
Lesson 1	Can (affirmative)		46
Lesson 2	Can't (negative)		48
Lesson 3	Can …? (questions and short answers)		50
Unit 8			
Lesson 1	Present continuous (affirmative)		52
Lesson 2	Present continuous (negative)		54
Lesson 3	Present continuous (questions and short answers)		56
Review: Units 7 – 8			58
Unit 9			
Lesson 1	What am/are/is … doing?		60
	Where am/are/is … going?		61
Lesson 2	Imperative (affirmative)		62
	Imperative (negative)		63
Lesson 3	Let's		64
Unit 10			
Lesson 1	Plurals (–es, –ies and irregular)		66
Lesson 2	Some, any		68
Lesson 3	Where is …? / Where are …? / Prepositions		70
Review: Units 9 – 10			72
Unit 11			
Lesson 1	Present simple (affirmative)		74
Lesson 2	Present simple (negative)		76
Lesson 3	Present simple (questions and short answers)		78
Unit 12			
Lesson 1	What do/does … do …?		80
Lesson 2	Wh– question words		82
Lesson 3	What time is it?		84
Review: Units 11 – 12			86

1 Lesson 1

1 Read.

A chick and **an** egg!

A/an

We put **a** before a word to talk about one person, animal or thing.
If the word begins with **a**, **e**, **i**, **o** or **u**, we use **an**.

a chick
an egg

2 Circle.

1 (**a**)/ **an** panda
2 **a** / **an** song
3 **a** / **an** octopus
4 **a** / **an** girl
5 **a** / **an** queen

6 **a** / **an** egg
7 **a** / **an** boy
8 **a** / **an** duck
9 **a** / **an** apple
10 **a** / **an** camel

3 Write *a* or *an*.

1 __an__ elephant
2 _____ dog
3 _____ car
4 _____ insect
5 _____ baby

6 _____ box
7 _____ father
8 _____ ant
9 _____ mother
10 _____ sister

4 Follow the words to the pictures.

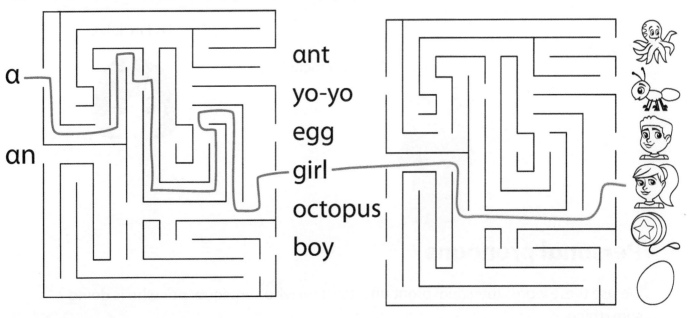

a

an

ant
yo-yo
egg
girl
octopus
boy

5 Say it!

An ant!

1 Read.

Hi, **I'm** Ana.

She's my friend!

Hi. **I'm** Sofia.

Personal pronouns

We use these words (personal pronouns) to show who someone is or who is doing something.

I   **you**   **he**   **she**   **it**   **we**   **you**   **they**

She is a nice girl.

It's a blue pencil.

2 Write.

he
he
it
~~I~~
she
they
we

CAT   brother   mum   DAD

I

3 Write.

~~boy~~	king
car	mum
dad	octopus
Emily	pencil
girl	sister
insect	Tom

he	she	it
boy	_____	_____
_____	_____	_____
_____	_____	_____
_____	_____	_____

4 Read.

To be (affirmative)

We use the verb **to be** to say who a person is or what a thing is. When we speak, we usually use the short form. We use **am** after **I**, **are** after **you**, and **is** after **he/she/it** or after the names of people and things.

I **am**	I'**m**
you **are**	you'**re**
he **is**	he'**s**
she **is**	she'**s**
it **is**	it'**s**

I **am** Sara.
You **are** Lucas.
Anabel **is** from Spain. She'**s** seven.
The cat **is** black.

5 Do the puzzle.

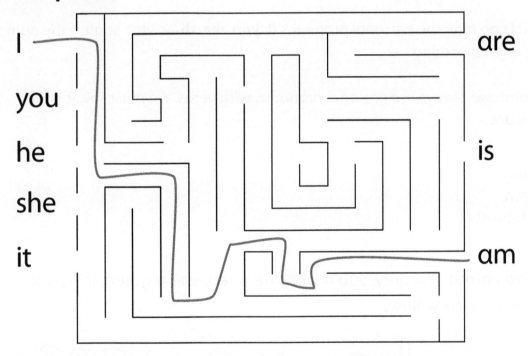

6 Circle.

1 My family **am** / **is** great.

2 You '**re** / '**s** my friend.

3 He **is** / **are** a boy.

4 Magda **is** / **am** my cousin.

5 Tomas **are** / **is** a baby.

6 I **am** / **is** cool!

7 It **am** / **is** an insect.

8 He '**s** / '**re** my uncle.

We're friends!

1 **Read.**

To be (affirmative)

We use the verb **to be** to say who a person is or what a thing is. When we speak, we usually use the short form.

I **am**	I'**m**
you **are**	you'**re**
he **is**	he'**s**
she **is**	she'**s**
it **is**	it'**s**
we **are**	we'**re**
you **are**	you'**re**
they **are**	they'**re**

Am, **are** and **is** go after the personal pronouns (**I**, **you**, **we**, **they**, etc.) or after the name of a person, animal or thing.

Note: In English we always use personal pronouns with verbs. We must say, for example, **we are**.

I **am** John.
Penny **is** a girl.
A frog **is** green.
Robots **are** fantastic!

2 **Match and colour.** (I = grey, you = blue, he = red, she = green, it = pink, we = purple, they = yellow)

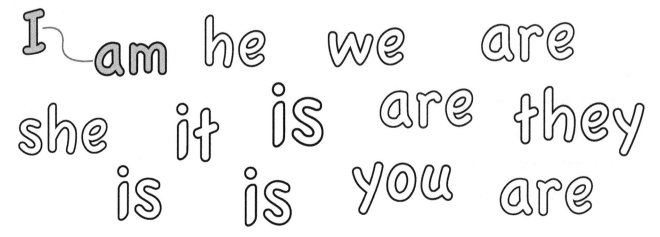

3 Circle.

1 Grandpa **is** / **are** cool.

2 I **am** / **is** seven.

3 Carlos **is** / **am** a boy.

4 Ana and Sofia **is** / **are** friends.

5 We **are** / **am** pupils.

6 You **are** / **is** fantastic!

7 They **are** / **is** babies.

8 It **am** / **is** an ant.

4 Write *am, are* or *is.*

My name (1) ___is___ Camila.

I (2) _____ seven. I'm from

Colombia. My sister (3) _____ four.

Look! My mum and dad (4) _____

in the photo, too. They (5) _____

cool! Grandma (6) _____ happy.

Grandpa (7) _____ happy, too.

We (8) _____ all happy.

5 Say it!

I'm Matilde. I'm eight.
I'm from Brazil. My sister is
Sabrina. She's five.
My mum and dad are nice.

Two dogs and one ball!

1 Read.

Plurals

To talk about more than one person, animal or thing, we usually add –s at the end of the word.

one sister → four sisters
one insect → two insects

2 Circle.

1 (hat)/ hats

2 insects / insect

3 candles / candle

4 photo / photos

5 house / houses

6 brother / brothers

3 Find and circle six words. Write.

emelephantsanafsyyoumonkeysandamonkeyisantsweantnaelephant

elephants

4 Write.

1 one ball   <u>seven balls</u>

3 one camera   _____

2 one bird   _____

4 one frog   _____

5 Say it!

Three dogs!

1 Read.

It's not a clock.
It's a puzzle.

To be (negative)

We put **not** after **am, are** and **is** to say who a person isn't or what a thing isn't.
When we speak, we usually use the short form.

I **am not**	I**'m not**
you **are not**	you **aren't**
he **is not**	he **isn't**
she **is not**	she **isn't**
it **is not**	it **isn't**
we **are not**	we **aren't**
you **are not**	you **aren't**
they **are not**	they **aren't**

You **aren't** funny.
They **aren't** short.

2 Circle.

1 She **is** / **isn't** a student.
She **is** / **isn't** a teacher.

2 It **is** / **isn't** a clock.
It **is** / **isn't** a map.

3 It **is** / **isn't** a desk.
It **is** / **isn't** a chair.

4 They **are** / **aren't** teachers.
They **are** / **aren't** students.

5 It **is** / **isn't** a board.
It **is** / **isn't** a map.

3 Write.

> ~~aren't~~   aren't   isn't   isn't   isn't   'm not

1 The chairs ___aren't___ blue. They're brown.

2 It _____ an ant. It's a worm.

3 They _____ boys. They're girls.

4 She's tall. She _____ short.

5 I _____ nine. I'm eight.

6 He's from Greece. He _____ from England.

4 Circle.

1

We ____ brothers.

a   aren't

b   are *(circled)*

2

He ____ happy.

a   is

b   isn't

3

She ____ a baby.

a   isn't

b   is

4

They ___ tall.

a   aren't

b   are

5

You ____ funny.

a   are

b   aren't

6

We ____ cool.

a   are

b   aren't

5 Say it!

> I'm not eight. I'm seven.
> I'm not short. I'm tall!
> My brother isn't tall.

Are you friends?

Yes, we are!

1 Read.

To be (questions and short answers)

To ask questions with **to be** we put **am, are** or **is** at the beginning of the question. We can give short answers with **Yes** or **No**, the person and **am, are** or **is**.

Am I ...?   **Is** it ...?

Are you ...?   **Are** we ...?

Is he ...?   **Are** you ...?

Is she ...?   **Are** they ...?

Are you a king?
Yes, I **am**. / No, I'm **not**.

Are they pencils?
Yes, they **are**. / No, they **aren't**.

2 Match.

1    Is it a pen?   **a**   Yes, he is.

2    Is he happy?   **b**   No, it isn't.

3    Are they sisters?   **c**   Yes, it is.

4    Are they camels?   **d**   No, they aren't.

5    Is it a birthday cake? **e**   Yes, they are.

3 Write *Am*, *Are* or *Is*.

1 _____Is_____ the toy small?

2 _____ the cakes yummy?

3 _____ Emily happy?

4 _____ I cool?

5 _____ you OK?

6 _____ we tall?

7 _____ it a pencil?

8 _____ she your mum?

4 Write.

1  Are you ten?

Yes, I am.

2 Is she short?

_____

3  Is it a mouse?

_____

4  Are they cakes?

_____

5  Are we friends?

_____

6  Is he a teacher?

_____

5 Say it!

Is it small?

Is it big?

Is it a hippo?

No, it isn't.

Yes, it is.

Yes, it is.

1 **Write.**

~~boy~~   egg   elephant   frog   hat   insect   parrot   umbrella

a	an
_____boy_____	_____
_____	_____
_____	_____
_____	_____

2 **Write _am_, _are_ or _is_.**

~~am~~   are   are   are   is   is

1 I _____am_____ Liz.

2 He _____ my brother.

3 We _____ friends.

4 They _____ boys.

5 It _____ an egg.

6 You _____ tall!

3 **Write.**

ant   duck   frog   hippo   insect   tiger

1 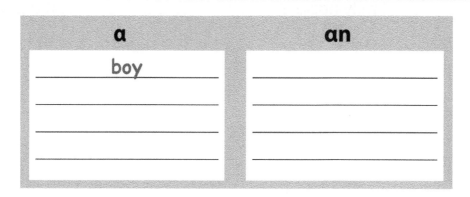 ___two tigers___

2 _____

3 _____

4  _____

5  _____

6 _____

4 Circle.

1 She **aren't** / **isn't** seven.

2 We **aren't** / **'m not** sad.

3 It **aren't** / **isn't** green.

4 I'm **not** / **aren't** a boy!

5 They **isn't** / **aren't** cool!

6 You **aren't** / **isn't** a baby!

5 Write.

1 _____Is_____ it small?
Yes, it _____is_____ .

2 _____ they short?
No, they _____ .

3 _____ she happy?
No, she _____ .

4 _____ he your dad?
Yes, he _____ .

5 _____ you brothers?
No, we _____ .

6 Look and write.

1 ___It's___ a board.
___It isn't___ a map.

2 Is it a pen? No, _____ .
_____ a pencil.

3 _____ rulers?
Yes, _____ .

4 _____ tall?
Yes, _____ .

5 _____ young?
No, _____ . They're old.

6 _____ a student?
No, _____ a teacher.

This is my cat and that's my dog.

1 Read.

This/that

We use **this** to point to a person, animal or thing which is near us. We use **that** to point to a person, animal or thing which is far away from us.

This is a rabbit.
That is a bird.
Note: There is a short form: **That is** → **That's**

2 Circle.

1 (This)/ That is a rabbit.
   This /(That) is a cat.

4 **This / That** is a sandwich.
   This / That is cake.

2 **This / That** is a lion.
   This / That is a monkey.

5 **This / That** is a bird.
   This / That is a dog.

3 **This / That** is a dolphin.
   This / That is a whale.

6 **This / That** is a computer game.
   This / That is a toy.

3 **Say it!** Write and colour. Then say.

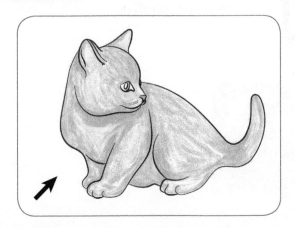

1 __This__ is a __grey__ cat.

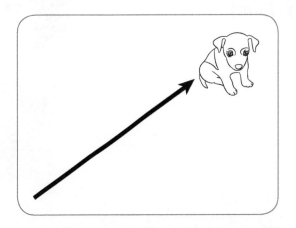

4 _____ is a _____ dog.

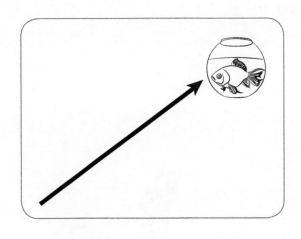

2 _____ is a _____ fish.

5 _____ is a _____ rabbit.

3 _____ is a _____ bird.

6 _____ is a _____ duck.

Lesson 2

1 Read.

These are zebras and those are giraffes.

These/those

To point to more than one person, animal or thing that is near us, we use **these**. We use the word **those** if they are far away from us.

These are rabbits.
Those are birds.

2 Write *these* or *those*.

1 __These__ are zebras and __those__ are monkeys.

3 _____ cakes are yummy, but _____ cakes aren't nice.

2 _____ are big eggs and _____ are small eggs.

4 _____ are ants and _____ are spiders.

3 Circle.

1 **That / Those** are ducks. *(Those is circled)*

2 **This / These** are frogs.

3 **This / Those** is an elephant.

4 **That / Those** are baby lions.

5 **This / These** is a tree.

6 **That / Those** is a giraffe.

4 Match.

1

2

This is a monkey.

These are monkeys.

That's a monkey.

Those are monkeys.

3

4

What are those?

They're sharks!

1 Read.

What's this/that? What are these/those?

We use **What** to ask about actions, animals, things, etc. To answer questions with **What …?** we use **It's** for one thing and **They're** for many things.

What is this?	**It's** a dolphin.
What is that?	**It's** a tree.
What are these?	**They're** toys.
What are those?	**They're** hats.

Note: There is a short form: **What is …?** ➔ **What's …?**

2 Choose and write.

~~It's~~   It's   It's   They're
They're   They're

an igloo   a robot   ~~a shark~~
dolphins   penguins   skateboards

1 What's that?
It's a shark.

4 What's this?
_____

2 What are these?
_____

5 What are those?
_____

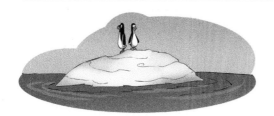

3 What are those?
_____

6 What's that?
_____

3 Write *What's* or *What are* and match.

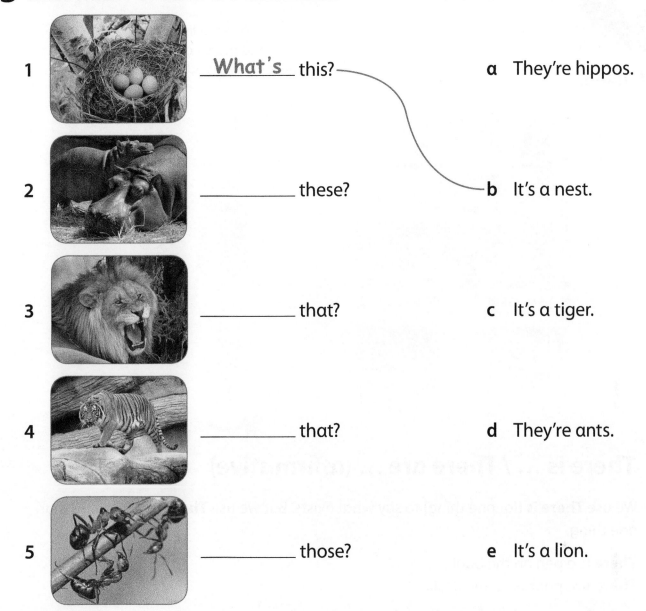

1 <u>What's</u> this?   **a** They're hippos.

2 _____ these?   **b** It's a nest.

3 _____ that?   **c** It's a tiger.

4 _____ that?   **d** They're ants.

5 _____ those?   **e** It's a lion.

4 **Say it!**

What's this?

It's a pen!

What are these?

They're books!

4 Lesson 1

1 Read.

> There's a living room
> and there's a bathroom.
> There are two beds in the bedroom.

There is … / There are … (affirmative)

We use **There is** (for one thing) to say what exists. But we use **There are** for more than one thing.

There is a pen on the book.
There are photos on the desk.

Note: There is a short form: **There is** ➡ **There's**

---

2 Circle. Then write *Yes* or *No*.

1 (**There are**) / **There is** bedrooms in the house.   ___Yes___

2 **There's** / **There are** an elephant in my bag.   _____

3 **There are** / **There's** a giraffe in the car.   _____

4 **There's** / **There are** dolphins in the sea.   _____

5 **There's** / **There are** a teacher in the classroom.   _____

6 **There are** / **There's** classrooms in the school.   _____

7 **There are** / **There's** boys and girls in my class.   _____

8 **There are** / **There's** zebras at our school.   _____

3 Look and read. Write *T* for True or *F* for False.

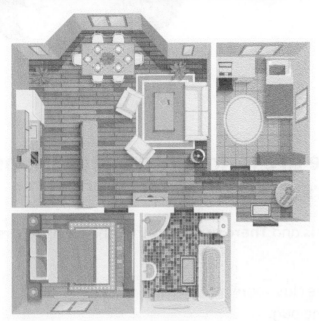

1 There is a kitchen. ☐ T

2 There are two bedrooms. ☐

3 There are two bathrooms. ☐

4 There is a garden. ☐

5 There is a living room. ☐

6 There are three cats in the living room. ☐

4 Write *there is* or *there are*. Then draw.

A picnic! **(1)** ___There are___ crisps. **(2)** _____ six green apples,

(3) _____ eight sandwiches, and **(4)** _____ a big bottle

of lemonade. Yummy! **(5)** _____ a big pink cake. Oh no!

(6) _____ three ants, too.

Is there a computer in the classroom?

No, there isn't.

1 Read.

There is ... / There are ... (negative, questions and short answers)

We put **n't** (**not**) after **There is** and **There are** to say that there isn't a person, animal or thing.

There isn't a computer in the classroom.
There aren't any books in the bag.

To ask if there is a person, animal or thing, we put **is** or **are** at the beginning of the question. We can give short answers with **Yes, there is/are** or **No, there isn't/aren't**.

Is there a computer on the desk?
Yes, **there is**. / No, **there isn't**.

Are there ten boys in your class?
Yes, **there are**. / No, **there aren't**.

2 Circle.

1 There **isn't** / **aren't** a TV in the living room.
2 There **isn't** / **aren't** 20 pencils in the box.
3 There **isn't** / **aren't** a snake in the tree.
4 There **isn't** / **aren't** elephants in Australia.
5 There **isn't** / **aren't** a photo in my bag.

3 Write.

1 There's one teacher in the classroom. (two teachers)
 There aren't two teachers in the classroom.

2 There's a spider on the desk. (an ant)
 _____

3 There are ten toys in the bedroom. (15 toys)
 _____

4 There's a lamp in the kitchen. (TV)
 _____

4 **Write about your school.**

1 ? / a cat / there / is

Is there a cat?

No, there isn't.

2 ? / is / a big tree / there

_____

_____

3 ? / girls / are / there

_____

_____

4 ? / toys / are / there

_____

_____

5 ? / there / is / a bus

_____

_____

6 ? / insects / there / are

_____

_____

7 ? / there / is / a TV

_____

_____

8 ? / are / drawings / there

_____

_____

5 **Say it!**

| beach | boys | car | cat | chairs | dog | flowers |
| girls | hat | houses | trees | umbrellas |

Is there a beach?

No, there isn't.

1 Read.

Look! The moon and a bird. The bird is an owl.

A, an, the

We use **a/an** to talk about one person, animal or thing. We use **the** instead of **a/an** to talk about a specific person, animal or thing, or to talk about it, or them, again.

Look! **A** helicopter. **The** helicopter is big.

We also use **the** to talk about something which is unique, for example, *the sky, the moon, the sun.*

The sun is yellow.
The sky is blue.

2 Write *a*, *an* or *the*.

1  _____an_____ ant

2  _____ sun

3  _____ egg

4  _____ book

5  _____ sky

6  _____ apple

7  _____ computer

8  _____ umbrella

9  _____ moon

10 _____ lamp

3 Circle.

1 (**The**) / **A** sun is yellow.

2 There's **a** / **the** big tree outside.

3 There's **the** / **a** bird in **the** / **a** sky.

4 Is this **a** / **the** blue pen?

5 That's **a** / **an** egg.

6 Look! It's **the** / **a** moon.

4 Write *a, an* or *the*.

1 There isn't _____a_____ bird in _____the_____ tree.

2 There are two dolphins in _____ sea. _____ dolphins are big.

3 That's _____ funny hat!

4 There's _____ cat in the garden! _____ cat is hungry.

5 That isn't _____ doll. It's _____ robot.

5 Write *a, an* or *the*. Then draw and colour.

In my bedroom, there is (1) _____a_____ green desk and (2) _____ blue chair. On (3) _____ desk, there is (4) _____ pen and two pencils. (5) _____ pen is black, and (6) _____ pencils are red and orange. There is (7) _____ notebook and two books. (8) _____ notebook is brown, and (9) _____ books are yellow. There is (10) _____ grey computer, too.

1 **Circle and write.**

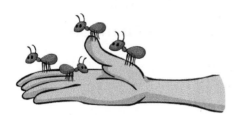

1 What are (these) / **those**?

_____They're_____ ants.

2 What are **these** / **those**?

_____ birds.

3 What's **this** / **that**?

_____ a snake.

4 What's **this** / **that**?

_____ a mountain.

5 What's **this** / **that**?

_____ a lizard.

6 What are **these** / **those**?

_____ lemons.

2 **Write.**

| Are | aren't | Is | Is | is | ~~isn't~~ | isn't |

1 There _____isn't_____ a TV in my bedroom.

2 _____ there books on the bed? No, there _____ .

3 _____ there an ant on the desk? Yes, there _____ !

4 _____ there a TV in the living room? No, there _____ .

3 Circle.

1  (There are) / There aren't seven candles.

2 There isn't / There is a girl.

3 There are / There aren't ten notebooks.

4  There isn't / There is a teddy bear.

5  There are / There aren't three monkeys.

6  There is / There isn't a pencil.

4 Tick (✔) or cross (✗).

1 There are two bathrooms. ___✗___

2 There is a living room. _____

3 There aren't three bedrooms. _____

4 There isn't a desk. _____

5 There isn't a chair in the kitchen. _____

6 There is a TV in the living room. _____

7 There is a lamp in the living room. _____

8 There aren't two lamps in the bedroom. _____

5 Write.

ant	computer	desk	elephant	moon
	photo	sea	sun	umbrella

a	an	the
computer		

Ants have got six legs.

1 Read.

Have got (affirmative)

We use **have got** to say that a thing belongs to a person or to describe a person or thing. When we speak, we usually use the short form.

I **have got**	I**'ve got**
you **have got**	you**'ve got**
he **has got**	he**'s got**
she **has got**	she**'s got**
it **has got**	it**'s got**
we **have got**	we**'ve got**
you **have got**	you**'ve got**
they **have got**	they**'ve got**

Have got and **has got** go after the personal pronouns (**I**, **you**, **he**, **she**, **it**, **we**, **they**) and after the name of a person, animal or thing.

I**'ve got** two brothers.
Paul**'s got** a computer.
The lion**'s got** a big head.
The robot **has got** four arms.

2 Write.

1 You have got a computer.   _____You've got_____ a computer.

2 He has got a funny cat.   _____ a funny cat.

3 It has got a big head.   _____ a big head.

4 They have got red pens.   _____ red pens.

5 You have got a brother.   _____ a brother.

6 She has got two rabbits.   _____ two rabbits.

7 We have got teddy bears.   _____ teddy bears.

8 I have got a computer.   _____ a computer.

3 Write *have got* or *has got*.

1 The robot _____ has got _____ four arms.

2 Birds _____ two legs.

3 Giraffes _____ long legs.

4 I _____ two brothers.

5 My sister _____ a doll.

6 We _____ three cousins.

4 Circle.

I (1) **'s got** /**'ve got** three cats.
They (2) **'s got** / **'ve got** white hair.
This is Mickey. Mickey (3) **'ve got /
's got** sad eyes, but he's happy!

This is a tarantula spider.
It (4) **'ve got** / **'s got** eight legs.
It (5) **'s got** / **'ve got** hair. These
spiders (6) **has got** / **have got**
big teeth, too.

5 **Say it!** Draw and say.

It's got a big head.
It's got two arms.
It's got four legs.

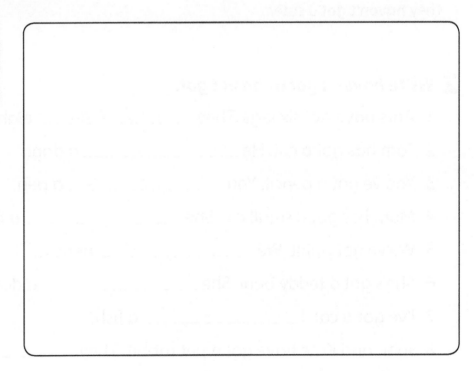

1 Read.

My robot hasn't got two legs. It's got one leg.

Have got (negative)

We put the word **not** after **have/has** to make the negative form. When we speak, we usually use the short form.

I **have not got**	I **haven't got**
you **have not got**	you **haven't got**
he **has not got**	he **hasn't got**
she **has not got**	she **hasn't got**
it **has not got**	it **hasn't got**
we **have not got**	we **haven't got**
you **have not got**	you **haven't got**
they **have not got**	they **haven't got**

I **haven't got** a dog.
They **haven't got** a sister.

2 Write *haven't got* or *hasn't got*.

1 Ants have got six legs. They ___haven't got___ eight legs.

2 Tom has got a cat. He _____ a dog.

3 You've got a pencil. You _____ a pen.

4 Mum has got a small car. She _____ a big car.

5 We've got paint. We _____ pencils.

6 She's got a teddy bear. She _____ a doll.

7 I've got a cat. I _____ a fish.

8 John and Kate have got a pet rabbit. They _____ a bird.

3 Circle.

1 They **have got** / **haven't got** toys.

2 The boys **hasn't got** / **haven't got** long hair.

3 The girl **'s got** / **hasn't got** a doll.

4 They **have got** / **haven't got** toy cars.

5 The girl **has got** / **hasn't got** long hair.

6 The girl **has got** / **hasn't got** a hat.

7 They **'ve got** / **haven't got** toy robots.

8 They **'ve got** / **haven't got** a computer.

4 Write *have got* or *haven't got*.

Hi, I'm Mary. This is my bag. My bag is yellow! I (1) _____have got_____ a rubber and a ruler in my bag.

I (2) _____ a book, but

I (3) _____ two notebooks.

I (4) _____ three pencils,

too. I (5) _____ a computer,

but I (6) _____ an apple

for my teacher.

1 Read.

Has your mum got long hair?

No, she hasn't.

Have got (questions and short answers)

We put **Have** or **Has** at the beginning of a question to ask if a person has got a thing.
We can give short answers with **Yes** or **No**, the person and **have/has** or **haven't/hasn't**.

Have I got ...?
Have you got ...?
Has he got ...?
Has she got ...?
Has it got ...?
Have we got ...?
Have you got ...?
Have they got ...?

Has Tom **got** a car?
Yes, he **has**. / No, he **hasn't**.

Have you **got** a TV?
Yes, we **have**. / No, we **haven't**.

Note: When **have** is in the question, we answer with **have** or **haven't**. When **has** is in the
question, we answer with **has** or **hasn't**. We don't use **got** in short answers.

2 Write *Have* or *Has*. Then match.

1 ___Has___ Annie got a teddy bear?   **a** No, I haven't.

2 _____ rabbits got long ears?   **b** Yes, she has.

3 _____ Max got a computer?   **c** Yes, he has.

4 _____ a worm got legs?   **d** No, it hasn't.

5 _____ you got wings?   **e** Yes, they have.

3 Write.

Marvin   **Bob**   **George**

1 Has Marvin got three arms?   _No, it hasn't._

2 Have the robots got wings?   _____

3 Has George got a big head?   _____

4 Has Marvin got four legs?   _____

5 Have the robots got arms?   _____

6 Has Bob got two eyes?   _____

4 Say it!

Have you got a pencil?

Yes, I have.

My new jumper is cool!

1 Read.

Possessive adjectives

We can use these words (possessive adjectives) to show whose something is.

my	**our**
your	**your**
his	**their**
her	
its	

Note: Possessive adjectives always go before the noun.
It's **her** mask.
Don't confuse **it's** = **it is** with the possessive adjective **its**.

2 Match and colour. (I = red, you = blue, he = grey, she = green, it = pink, we = purple, they = yellow)

he   her   his   it   I
she   their   its   we
they   our   your   my   you

3 Circle.

1 She's got a new skirt. **His /** (**Her**) skirt is red.

2 Mario and Leo are twins. **His / Their** birthday is today.

3 Elsa's brother's got a cool hat. **Her / His** hat is purple and yellow.

4 My parents and I have got new jackets. **Your / Our** jackets are warm.

5 I've got one cat. **Its / Her** tail is very long.

6 Have you got a cat in **our / your** house?

4 Match.

1 I've got a new 🧣 .

2 She's got new 👢 .

3 He's got new 👢 , too.

4 They've got new 👕 .

5 My dog's got a ⚫ .

a His boots are green.

b My scarf is long.

c Her boots are yellow.

d Its ball is big.

e Their T-shirts are green.

5 Write.

1 Look at that dog! _____Its_____ Its tail is white.

2 They're funny cats. _____ ears are small.

3 We're sisters. _____ dresses are green.

4 Ana is cool. _____ jeans are new.

5 You're wet! _____ umbrella is old.

6 That's an elephant. _____ nose is long.

6 Say it! Colour and write. Then say.

This is _____ .

_____ hair is

_____ .

_____ jumper is

_____ .

This is _____ .

_____ hair is

_____ .

_____ jumper is

_____ .

1 Read.

These are Dad's socks and this is Mum's hat.

Possessive 's

We put **'s** after the name of a person to show who a thing belongs to.

It's **Kathy's** mobile phone.

They're **Billy's** shoes.

We can also put **'s** after a person (**I**, **you**, **he**, etc.) or animal to show who owns something.

It's **Dad's** shirt.

They're the **dog's** toys.

2 Write.

1 _____Paul's_____ notebook

2 _____ book

3 _____ pen

4 _____ pencil

5 _____ rubber

3 Write.

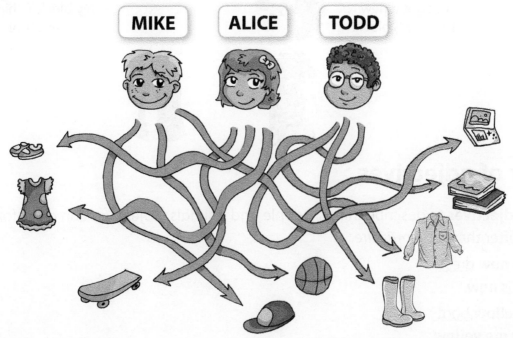

MIKE   ALICE   TODD

1 They're ___Todd's___ boots.

2 It's _____ hat.

3 It's _____ dress.

4 It's _____ computer game.

5 They're _____ books.

6 They're _____ shoes.

7 It's _____ shirt.

8 It's _____ skateboard.

9 It's _____ ball.

4 Write.

1 Mum / hat
   __It's Mum's hat.__

2 Jack / scarf
   _____

3 the cat / toy
   _____

4 Doris / T-shirt
   _____

5 my sister / hat
   _____

6 your brother / ball
   _____

1 Read.

I've got a new T-shirt. It's black.

My black T-shirt is new, too!

Order of adjectives

We use **adjectives** to describe things, people and animals. Adjectives can go before a noun or after the verb *am/is/are*.

I've got a **new** dress.
My dress is **new**.

I've got **yellow** boots.
My boots are **yellow**.

My **new** boots are **black**.
My **black** boots are **new**.

2 Cross out one word.

1 I've got new boots new.
2 My new boots cool are cool.
3 This apple yummy is yummy.
4 My hat cool is cool.

5 I've got yellow boots yellow.
6 My dog's got a short tail short.
7 Your socks funny are funny.
8 My new jumper new is black.

3 Write.

1 She's got __new shoes__ . (👟) (new)

2 His _____ are _____ . (👖) (grey)

3 Your _____ is _____ . (👗) (orange)

4 She's got a _____ _____ . (👗) (pretty)

5 Our new _____ are _____ . (👢) (yellow)

4 Write and colour.

1 are / trousers / Marco's / blue
  Marco's trousers are blue.

2 He's / orange / got / T-shirt / an
  _____

3 is / hat / His / yellow and red
  _____

4 He's / balloon / a / purple / got
  _____

5 hair / got / Lara's / long
  _____

6 green / dress / is / Her
  _____

7 brown / are / shoes / Her
  _____

8 a / balloon / got / She's / red
  _____

MARCO   LARA

Review

1 Write **have got, has got, haven't got** or **hasn't got.**

1 Elephants _____have got_____ big ears. (✔)

2 Giraffes _____ short legs. (✗)

3 My baby sister _____ a toy car. (✗)

4 My schoolbag _____ books and pencils in it. (✔)

5 A snake _____ any hands. (✗)

6 We _____ new hats. (✔)

2 Write.

1 _____Has_____ your brother got a hat?   Yes, _____he has_____ .

2 _____ spiders got eight legs?   Yes, _____ .

3 _____ your dog got a black nose?   Yes, _____ .

4 _____ a fish got legs?   No, _____ .

5 _____ cats got fingers?   No, _____ .

3 Tick (✔) or cross (✗).

1 She's got a skirt.   _✗_

2 She hasn't got a hat.   _____

3 She hasn't got a toy robot.   _____

4 The robot hasn't got any legs.   _____

5 The robot's got eyes.   _____

6 The girl and the robot have got arms. _____

7 The robot hasn't got a coat.   _____

8 The girl has got socks.   _____

4 Circle and colour.

Lisa	Tom

1 **Lisa's / Tom's** umbrella is red.

2 **Lisa's / Tom's** shoes are brown.

3 **Her / His** boots are yellow.

4 **Her / His** hair is long and brown.

5 **Her / His** hair is short and black.

6 **Their / Our** clothes are cool!

5 Write.

her	his	its	my	our	their	your

1 We put _____ our _____ books in the bookcase.

2 _____ name is Angela. What's _____ name?

3 Laura has got a brother. _____ name is Brandon.

4 Has Helen got a computer in _____ bedroom?

5 This is a rabbit. _____ ears are big.

6 The children are in _____ classroom.

I can speak English.

1 Read.

Can (affirmative)

We use the word **can** and a verb to say what we are able to do.

I **can cook**.
You **can cook**.
He **can cook**.
She **can cook**.
It **can cook**.
We **can cook**.
You **can cook**.
They **can cook**.

2 Tick (✔) or cross (✗).

1 Worms can run. ☒

2 Parrots can speak. ☐

3 Cats can cook. ☐

4 Dolphins can swim. ☐

5 My teacher can speak English. ☐

6 Babies can read. ☐

7 Dogs and cats can speak. ☐

8 We can listen to music. ☐

9 Birds can sing. ☐

3 Write.

cook   ~~jump~~   read   run   swim   write

1  They __can jump__ .

2  She _____ .

3  They _____ .

4 They _____ .

5 They _____ .

6 They _____ .

4 **Say it!**   **Draw and colour. Then say.**

I can swim. My sister can swim, too.

1 Read.

I can't speak Spanish.

Can't (negative)

We use **cannot** or **can't** to say what we are not able to do. We usually use the short form.

I **cannot sing**.	I **can't sing**.
You **cannot sing**.	You **can't sing**.
He **cannot sing**.	He **can't sing**.
She **cannot sing**.	She **can't sing**.
It **cannot sing**.	It **can't sing**.
We **cannot sing**.	We **can't sing**.
You **cannot sing**.	You **can't sing**.
They **cannot sing**.	They **can't sing**.

2 Circle.

1 Bears (can) / **can't** run, but they **can** / (**can't**) read.

2 An octopus **can** / **can't** swim, but it **can** / **can't** speak.

3 Dolphins **can** / **can't** play with a ball, but they **can** / **can't** sit down.

4 A fish **can** / **can't** dance, but it **can** / **can't** swim.

3 Write.

	dance	sing	paint	draw
Patricio	✔	✘	✘	✔
Isabella	✘	✔	✔	✘
Celeste	✔	✔	✘	✔

1 Patricio ____can't____ sing.

2 Isabella and Celeste _____ sing.

3 Celeste and Patricio _____ draw.

4 Patricio _____ sing, but he _____ dance.

5 Isabella _____ paint, but she _____ draw.

6 Celeste _____ paint, but she _____ draw.

4 Write *can* or *can't*.

1

My teacher ____can____ read,
but she ____can't____ draw.

2

My dog _____ jump,
but it _____ swim.

3

Tara _____ dance,
but she _____ sing.

4
My brother _____ speak,
but he _____ walk.

5 **Say it!** Tick (✔) or cross (✗). Then say.

	dance	sing	paint	draw	swim	cook
I						
_____						
_____						

1 Read.

Can you draw?

Can you paint?

Yes, I can.

No, I can't.

Can ...? (questions and short answers)

We put **Can** at the beginning of a question to ask if a person is able to do an action. We answer with **Yes** or **No**, the person and **can** or **can't**.

Can I **sing**?	Yes, I **can**. / No, I **can't**.
Can you **sing**?	Yes, you **can**. / No, you **can't**.
Can he **sing**?	Yes, he **can**. / No, he **can't**.
Can she **sing**?	Yes, she **can**. / No, she **can't**.
Can it **sing**?	Yes, it **can**. / No, it **can't**.
Can we **sing**?	Yes, we **can**. / No, we **can't**.
Can you **sing**?	Yes, you **can**. / No, you **can't**.
Can they **sing**?	Yes, they **can**. / No, they **can't**.

2 Match.

1 Can a lion draw?   **a** No, it can't.

2 Can Ana and Carlos dance?   **b** Yes, he can.

3 Can Frank sing?   **c** No, they can't.

4 Can a dolphin swim?   **d** Yes, she can.

5 Can you read?   **e** Yes, I can.

6 Can Lucy dance?   **f** Yes, it can.

3 Answer about you.

1 Can you play the drums?   <u>Yes, I can. / No, I can't.</u>

2 Can your mum jump?   _____

3 Can your dad swim?   _____

4 Can you play volleyball?   _____

5 Can you dance?   _____

6 Can your teacher play the guitar? _____

4 Write.

1 ? / Sam / can / read / ✗

   <u>Can Sam read?</u>

   <u>No, he can't.</u>

2 ? / the boys / jump / can / ✔

   _____

   _____

3 ? / swim / Kim / can / ✗

   _____

   _____

4 ? / dance / can / your friends / ✔

   _____

   _____

5 ? / the piano / play / can / Harry / ✗

   _____

   _____

6 ? / play / the drums / can / Kathy / ✔

   _____

   _____

5 Say it!

Can parrots walk?

Yes, they can.

	Parrots	Snakes
walk	✔	✗
fly	✔	✗
climb	✔	✔
swim	✗	✔
eat frogs	✗	✔

I'm playing tennis.

8 Lesson 1

1 Read.

Present continuous (affirmative)

To talk about an action which is happening now, we use the **present continuous**. We form this tense with **am/are/is** + verb + **–ing**. When we speak, we usually use the short form.

I **am** cook**ing**.	I**'m** cook**ing**.
You **are** cook**ing**.	You**'re** cook**ing**.
He **is** cook**ing**.	He**'s** cook**ing**.
She **is** cook**ing**.	She**'s** cook**ing**.
It **is** cook**ing**.	It**'s** cook**ing**.
We **are** cook**ing**.	We**'re** cook**ing**.
You **are** cook**ing**.	You**'re** cook**ing**.
They **are** cook**ing**.	They**'re** cook**ing**.

Note: When the verb ends in **–e**, we drop the **–e** before adding **–ing**.

dance	They're danc**ing**.
write	We're writ**ing.**

When the verb has got only one syllable and ends in **consonant-vowel-consonant**, we double the consonant at the end of the verb.

sit	She's sit**ting**.

2 Write.

1 They are reading.
   They're reading.

2 He is sitting.
   _____

3 We are singing.
   _____

4 I am writing.
   _____

5 You are watching TV.
   _____

6 It is running.
   _____

7 She is sleeping.
   _____

8 They are playing tennis.
   _____

3 Match.

1

She's playing a game.

He's watching TV.

4

They're riding their bikes.

2

You're reading!

5

It's eating.

3

They're dancing.

6

4 Write.

eat
listen
play
~~read~~
sleep
watch

1 Grandpa ____is reading____ a book.

2 Tom and Lucy _____ a video game.

3 Dad _____ TV.

4 The cat _____ on the floor.

5 Mum and Grandma _____ apples.

6 Meg _____ to music.

1 Read.

I'm not playing tennis!

Present continuous (negative)

We use the **present continuous** with **not** after **am**, **are**, **is** to say that a person is not doing an action now. When we speak, we usually use the short form.

I **am not** cook**ing**.	I**'m not** cook**ing**.
You **are not** cook**ing**.	You **aren't** cook**ing**.
He **is not** cook**ing**.	He **isn't** cook**ing**.
She **is not** cook**ing**.	She **isn't** cook**ing**.
It **is not** cook**ing**.	It **isn't** cook**ing**.
We **are not** cook**ing**.	We **aren't** cook**ing**.
You **are not** cook**ing**.	You **aren't** cook**ing**.
They **are not** cook**ing**.	They **aren't** cook**ing**.

2 Circle.

1 The cat **isn't** / **aren't** sleeping.

2 They **isn't** / **aren't** playing the drums.

3 You **aren't** / **isn't** listening.

4 We **isn't** / **aren't** running.

5 I **aren't** / **'m not** singing.

6 She **isn't** / **aren't** watching TV.

3 Write.

1 I'm reading a book. (not write)

I'm not writing.

2 Sam is watching TV. (not sleep)

_____

3 Pip and Susie are playing tennis. (not play football)

_____

4 We are singing a song. (not listen to music)

_____

5 The cat is eating its food. (not run)

_____

4 Write.

| eat | kick | play | play | read | ~~throw~~ |

1 She _____isn't_____ hitting a ball.
She _____'s throwing_____ a ball.

4 She _____ eating an egg.
She _____ an apple.

2 He _____ playing baseball.
He _____ basketball.

5 They _____ playing baseball.
They _____ football.

3 He _____ catching a ball.
He _____ a ball.

6 They _____ writing on the board.
They _____ books.

1 Read.

Are you singing?

Yes, I am.

Present continuous (questions and short answers)

To ask if a person is doing an action now, we put **Am**, **Are**, **Is** at the beginning of the question. We can answer with **Yes** or **No**, the person and **am**, **are** or **is**.

Am I cook**ing**?	Yes, I **am**. / No, I'**m not**.
Are you cook**ing**?	Yes, you **are**. / No, you **aren't**.
Is he cook**ing**?	Yes, he **is**. / No, he **isn't**.
Is she cook**ing**?	Yes, she **is**. / No, she **isn't**.
Is it cook**ing**?	Yes, it **is**. / No, it **isn't**.
Are we cook**ing**?	Yes, we **are**. / No, we **aren't**.
Are you cook**ing**?	Yes, you **are**. / No, you **aren't**.
Are they cook**ing**?	Yes, they **are**. / No, they **aren't**.

2 Write.

1 Is he playing tennis?
Yes, he is.

2 Are they writing?
_____

3 Is she reading a book?
_____

4 Are they playing basketball?
_____

3 Write. Answer about you with a tick (✔) or cross (✗).

1 ? / your teacher / is / dancing
  <u>Is your teacher dancing?</u> ☒

2 ? / your friends / playing / are
  _____ ☐

3 ? / you / are / writing
  _____ ☐

4 ? / thinking / are / you
  _____ ☐

5 ? / the students / sitting / are
  _____ ☐

6 ? / a bird / is / singing
  _____ ☐

7 ? / your friend / reading / is
  _____ ☐

8 ? / losing / your team / is
  _____ ☐

4 Write.

1 <u>Is</u> he <u>playing</u> basketball? (play)
  <u>Yes, he is.</u>

2 _____ he _____ the ball? (throw)
  _____

3 _____ she _____ ? (cook)
  _____

4 _____ they _____ ? (have fun)
  _____

5 _____ he _____ ? (jump)
  _____

1 Write *can* or *can't*.

1 He ___can___ jump.

2 She _____ swim.

3 They _____ sing.

4 They _____ run.

5 It _____ read.

6 We _____ dance.

2 Look and write.

	Lyn	Alan	Maya	Philip
dance	✔			
play football	✔		✔	
swim	✔	✔		✔
sing	✔			
play the piano			✔	✔

1 ___Can___ Alan sing?   ___No, he can't.___

2 _____ Lyn and Maya play football?   _____

3 _____ Philip swim?   _____

4 _____ Lyn dance?   _____

5 _____ Lyn and Alan play the piano?   _____

6 _____ Philip and Lyn swim?   _____

3 **Write and answer about you.**

1 __Are__ you sleeping?   No, I'm not.

2 _____ your mum working?   _____

3 _____ your friends playing?   _____

4 _____ you writing?   _____

5 _____ your teacher standing?   _____

4 **Write and match.**

1 She ___is painting___ (paint).   **a**

2 They _____ (swim).   **b**

3 They _____ (play) the piano.   **c**

4 He _____ (kick) the ball.   **d**

5 **Answer about you.**

1 Can you read?

   Yes, I can. / No, I can't.

2 Are you reading now?

   _____

3 Can your teacher speak English?

   _____

4 Is your teacher speaking English now?

   _____

5 Can your friends play football?

   _____

6 Are your friends playing football now?

   _____

9 Lesson 1

What are you doing?

I'm reading about penguins.

1 Read.

What am/are/is ... doing?

We use **What** at the beginning of a question to ask what a person is doing now, or when we can see what a person is doing, but we want to ask more about the action.

What am I **doing?**
What are you **doing?**

What's he/she/it **doing?**
What are they **doing?**

What's = What is

2 Match.

1 What are you doing?
2 What am I doing?
3 What is she doing?
4 What are they doing?
5 What are we doing?
6 What is he doing?
7 What is the cat doing?

a They're eating cake.
b I'm watching TV.
c We're having fun.
d She's playing the piano.
e You're playing basketball.
f It's running.
g He's watching TV.

3 Say it!

- read a book
- dance
- eat
- play basketball
- play tennis
- write
- sing
- sleep
- swim
- watch TV

What am I doing?

No, I'm not.

Yes, I am!

Are you swimming?

Are you dancing?

4 Read.

Where are you going?

I'm going to school.

Where am/are/is … going?

We use **Where** at the beginning of a question to ask where a person is going.
We use **to +** place in the answer.

Where am I **going?**
Where are you **going?**

Where's he/she/it **going?**
Where are they **going?**

I'm going **to** the theatre.

Where's = Where is

5 Write.

1 she / go
   Where is she going?

   she / go / theatre
   She's going to the theatre.

2 they / go
   _____

   they / go / museum
   _____

3 you / go
   _____

   I / go / library
   _____

4 we / go
   _____

   we / go / zoo
   _____

6 Say it!

you
he
she
we
they

Where is she going?

She's going to the cinema.

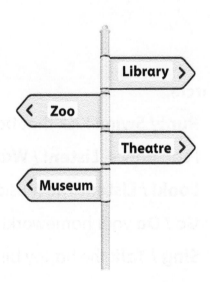

Library
Zoo
Theatre
Museum

1 Read.

Look! This house is cool!

Imperative (affirmative)

To give instructions or orders, we only use the verb for the action. It doesn't matter how many people we are talking to.

Stand up!

2 Match.

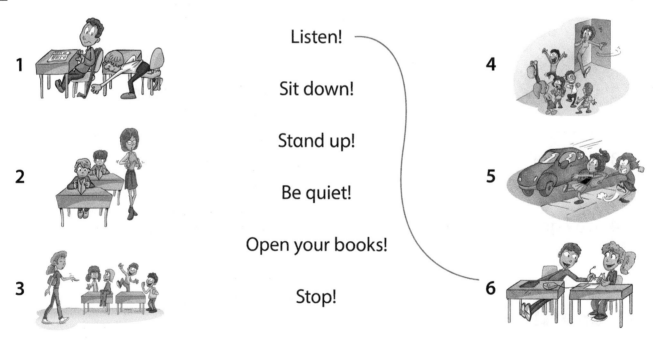

1

2

3

Listen!

Sit down!

Stand up!

Be quiet!

Open your books!

Stop!

4

5

6

3 Circle.

1 (Run!) / **Swim!** Kick that ball!

2 I can dance. **Listen! / Watch!**

3 **Look! / Listen!** The music is great!

4 **Go / Do** your homework!

5 **Sing / Talk** the happy birthday song!

4 Read.

Don't go to the playground!

Imperative (negative)

To tell a person not to do an action, we put **Don't** at the beginning of the sentence and before the verb.

Don't jump on the bed!

Don't = Do not

5 Write.

eat
go
play
sit
~~watch~~
write

House Rules:

1 ___Don't watch___ TV today!

2 _____ on Grandma's chair!

3 _____ football in the living room!

4 _____ on my book!

5 _____ to the toy shop!

6 _____ the cake!

6 Match.

1 Look at that cat!
2 Kick that ball!
3 Don't write on that book!
4 Listen to me!
5 Wear your hat!

a It's cold outside.
b I'm talking to you.
c It's beautiful.
d Your team can win.
e It's my book!

7 Write.

1 Talk to the teacher. ___Don't talk___ to your friends.

2 Don't run in the classroom. _____ in the playground.

3 Look at the board. _____ at your book.

4 Write with a pencil. _____ with a pen.

5 _____ happy. Don't be sad.

6 Don't swim in the sea. _____ in the pool.

1 **Read.**

Let's go to the cinema!

No. Let's go to the playground!

Let's

To suggest an action to other people, we use **Let's** at the beginning of the sentence and before the verb.

Let's run!

Let's = Let us

2 **Match.**

1 It's my birthday.   a Let's have a sandwich!

2 I'm hungry.   b Let's eat cake!

3 That's our teacher.   c Let's say hello!

4 I've got a new football.   d Let's swim!

5 This is a nice song.   e Let's sing!

6 The pool is warm.   f Let's play!

3 Write.

1 let's / the / playground / go / to

   <u>Let's go to the playground.</u>

2 read / let's / books / these

   _____

3 theatre / let's / to / go / the

   _____

4 toy shop / let's / robot / a / buy / at the

   _____

5 in the / take / let's / photos / park

   _____

6 the / go / let's / museum / new / to

   _____

4 Say it!

Let's draw!

No. Let's listen to music.

Look at the mice.
They're babies.

1 Read.

Plurals (–es, –ies and irregular)

When we talk about more than one person, animal or thing, we usually put –**s** at the end of the word.

one goat   →   two goat**s**

But when words end in –**s**, we put –**es** at the end of the word.

one bus   →   two bus**es**

The same happens when words end in –**ss, –ch, –sh, –x**.

one dress   →   five dress**es**
one beach   →   six beach**es**
one dish   →   four dish**es**
one box   →   two box**es**

We also put –**es** after some words that end in –**o**.

one potato   →   two potato**es**
one tomato   →   three tomato**es**

When words end in a consonant + –**y**, we drop the –**y** and we add –**ies**.

one baby   →   three babi**es**

But when words end in a vowel + –**y**, we add only –**s**.

one toy   →   ten toy**s**

There are some words which have a different form in the plural.

child	→	child**ren**	mouse	→	m**ice**
foot	→	f**ee**t	tooth	→	t**ee**th
man	→	m**e**n	woman	→	wom**e**n

2 Write.

1 one dress → two ___dresses___
2 one family → four _____
3 one monkey → three _____
4 one boy → six _____
5 one box → five _____
6 one mouse → seven _____
7 one child → four _____
8 one foot → two _____

3 Write.

baby bike bus cherry child city dish face family foot
fox man match mouse octopus party pen shirt strawberry
tomato tooth toy woman zebra

–s	–es	–ies	!
bikes	buses	babies	children

4 Read.

The 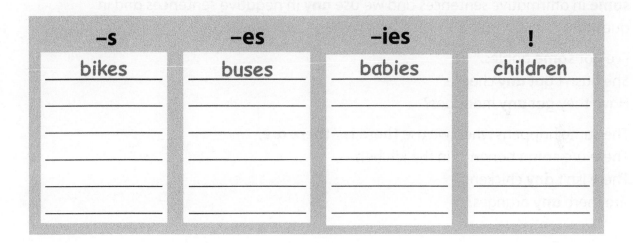 , the and the are looking at the

 .

1 **Read.**

I've got some bananas, but I haven't got any apples.

Some, any

To talk about an amount of people, animals or things we use **some** and **any**. We use **some** in affirmative sentences and we use **any** in negative sentences and in questions.

I've got **some** apples.
She hasn't got **any** cheese.
Have they got **any** mangoes?

The same happens when we use **there is / there are**.
There are **some** bananas in the kitchen.
There isn't **any** chicken.
Are there **any** oranges?

2 **Write some or any.**

1 There are ____some____ notebooks on the desk.

2 Lucy hasn't got _____ toys in her bag.

3 The boys haven't got _____ green pens, but they have got
_____ blue pens.

4 I've got _____ pencils, but I haven't got _____ rubbers.

5 Grandma's got _____ bananas and _____ apples for us.

6 There aren't _____ children in the park.

3 **Match.**

1 Has a dog got
2 There is
3 I've got
4 Look! There are
5 Have worms got
6 There aren't

a some oranges and some mangoes.
b any teeth?
c some cheese on the table.
d any toys?
e any apples in the kitchen.
f some bananas in the bag.

4 **Write *have got, haven't got, has got* or *hasn't got* with *some* or *any*.**

1 She __has got some__ apples.

3 The baby _____ milk.

2 We _____ books.

4 The dog _____ water.

5 **Say it!** **Choose three things you've got. Ask and answer.**

apples   chicken   juice   mangoes   milk   oranges   strawberries

Have you got
any apples?

Yes, I've got
some apples.

1 Read.

> The cat is in the basket.

Where is …? / Where are …? / Prepositions

When we ask about the place a person, animal or thing is, we use **Where is …?**
We use **Where are …?** for many people, animals or things.

Where is the apple?
Where are the apples?

Note: There is a short form: **Where is → Where's**

We use **prepositions of place** to say where a person, animal or thing is.

on
The apple is **on** the box.

behind
The apple is **behind** the box.

in
The apple is **in** the box.

in front of
The apple is **in front of** the box.

under
The apple is **under** the box.

next to
The apple is **next to** the box.

2 Write.

behind	in	~~in front of~~	next to	on	under

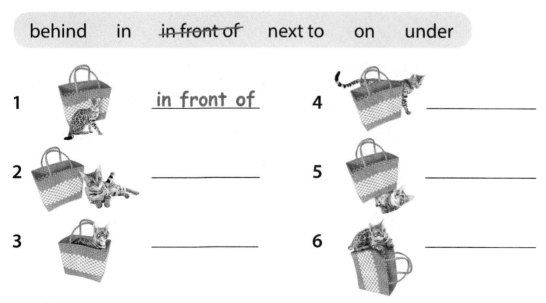

1 in front of

2 _____

3 _____

4 _____

5 _____

6 _____

3 Write *Where is* or *Where are* and a preposition. Then match.

1  <u>Where are</u> my shoes? a She's _____ the kitchen.

2  _____ the cheese? b They're _____ <u>behind</u> _____ the door.

3 _____ Tamsin? c They're _____ the box.

4  _____ the sweets? d It's _____ the table.

5  _____ the apples? e They're _____ the cake.

4 **Say it!**

- apples/bananas
- basket/door
- carrots/potatoes
- cat/chair
- man/chair
- pencil/notebook
- potatoes/basket
- tomatoes/carrots

Where are the apples?

They're next to the bananas.

Review

1 Write.

> have fun   go to the park   go to the playground
> ~~play football~~   play tennis   play the guitar

1 ___What are they___ doing?
They ___'re playing football___ .

4 _____ doing?
She _____ .

2 _____ doing?
They _____ .

5 _____ going?
We _____ .

3 _____ going?
She _____ .

6 _____ doing?
He _____ .

2 Match.

1 Don't eat   a at me!

2 Let's draw   b a picture!

3 Look   c to sleep!

4 Clean   d your shoes!

5 Don't go   e my sweets!

3 Write.

baby	~~dress~~	strawberry	student	tooth

1 Mary has got five red _____dresses_____ .

2 There are 20 _____ in my class.

3 I'm eating _____ .

4 _____ drink milk.

5 Our _____ are white.

4 Look and write *have got* or *haven't got* with *some* and *any*.

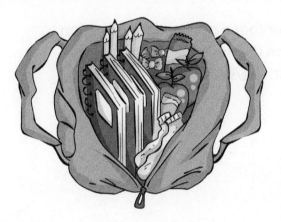

What's in my bag? I (1) ___have got some___
notebooks. I (2) _____ books.
I (3) _____ pens, but
I (4) _____ pencils.
I (5) _____ sweets and
I (6) _____ apples. Oh no!
I (7) _____ socks, too!
Are there any socks in your bag?

5 Write.

behind	in	~~in front of~~	next to	on	under

1 _____Where is_____ Sally?

She's ___in front of___ the door.

2 _____ Tom?

He's _____ the door.

3 _____ the chair?

It's _____ the door.

4 _____ Tom's shoes?

They're _____ the chair.

5 _____ Tom's bag?

It's _____ the chair.

6 _____ Tom's hat?

It's _____ the bag.

7 _____ Tom's socks?

They're _____ the bag.

11 Lesson 1

I like flowers!

1 Read.

Present simple (affirmative)

We use the **present simple** to say what happens, or that a person does an action *always, often, every day* or *usually*. We use the person (**I**, **you**, **we**, etc.) and the verb only in affirmative sentences. The verb changes with **he/she/it**. Then we must add –**s** at the end of the verb.

I swim
you swim
he swim**s**
she swim**s**
it swim**s**
we swim
you swim
they swim

I **like** chocolate.
He **climbs** big trees.

When the verb ends in –**sh**, –**ch**, –**o** and we have **he/she/it**, we add –**es** at the end of the verb.

Mike watch**es** TV.

When the verb ends in a consonant + –**y** and we have **he/she/it**, we drop the –**y** and we add –**ies** at the end of the verb.

Marco stud**ies** English.

2 Circle.

1 Mum **play** / **plays** tennis.

2 You **cook** / **cooks** dinner.

3 Aisha and Lee **walk** / **walks** to school.

4 We **sing** / **sings** songs at school.

5 Lee **like** / **likes** ice cream.

6 I **play** / **plays** football.

3 Write.

1 Aisha and Amira _____eat_____ (eat) apples and oranges.

2 I _____ (play) hockey.

3 Jason _____ (sit) next to Tom.

4 My brother _____ (catch) the ball.

5 Mae's sister _____ (listen) to great music!

6 You _____ (run) very fast!

7 My brother _____ (read) books about cats.

8 Rick _____ (do) his homework.

4 Write and match.

go   play   sit   study   watch   ~~win~~

1 Max _____wins_____ the cup every year.   a

2 Tom _____ next to Elliot at school.   b

3 Marta _____ hard at school.   c

4 Flo _____ to school on the bus.   d

5 I _____ the guitar.   e

6 Celeste _____ TV.   f

1 Read.

I like cold milk.
I don't like hot milk.

Present simple (negative)

To say that an action doesn't happen or that a person doesn't do an action *always, often, every day* or *usually*, we use the **present simple** with **do not** (**don't**) or **does not** (**doesn't**) before the verb.

We use **does not** with **he/she/it**, and with **I/you/we/you/they** we use **do not**. When we have **does not** (**doesn't**), we don't add **–s**, **–es** or **–ies** at the end of the verb.

When we speak, we usually use the short form.

I **do not** swim	I **don't** swim
you **do not** swim	you **don't** swim
he **does not** swim	he **doesn't** swim
she **does not** swim	she **doesn't** swim
it **does not** swim	it **doesn't** swim
we **do not** swim	we **don't** swim
you **do not** swim	you **don't** swim
they **do not** swim	they **don't** swim

She **doesn't** eat sweets.
They **don't** play tennis.

2 Circle.

1 I **don't** / **doesn't** go to school at the weekend.

2 He **don't** / **doesn't** play basketball.

3 We **don't** / **doesn't** go to the theatre.

4 My cat **don't** / **doesn't** eat bread.

5 Mum and Dad **don't** / **doesn't** watch TV.

6 She **don't** / **doesn't** sing very well!

3 Write.

climb   eat   go   play   ~~wear~~

1   Mum _____wears_____ trousers.
    She ___doesn't wear___ dresses.

2   Dad _____ sweets.
    He _____ popcorn.

3   They _____ basketball.
    They _____ tennis.

4   I _____ mountains.
    I _____ trees.

5   We _____ to the theatre.
    We _____ to the cinema.

4 Say it!

> My sister plays football. She doesn't play tennis.

I	eat	basketball hot milk
you	go	bread library
we	like	cheese oranges
my sister/brother	play	chocolate tennis
my friend		cold milk theatre
my friends		football strawberries
		hockey sweets

1 Read.

Do you play basketball in winter?

No, I don't.

Present simple (questions and short answers)

To form a question with the **present simple**, we put **Do** or **Does** at the beginning of the question. When we use **does**, we don't add **–s**, **–es** or **–ies** at the end of the verb. We can give short answers with **Yes** or **No**, the person and **do/does** or **don't/doesn't**.

Do I swim?
Do you swim?
Does he swim?
Does she swim?
Does it swim?
Do we swim?
Do you swim?
Do they swim?

Do you **like** oranges?
Yes, I **do**. / No, I **don't**.

Does Peter **play** hockey?
Yes, he **does**. / No, he **doesn't**.

2 Match.

1 Does Dean like computers?   a Yes, we do.
2 Does Laura go to school?   b No, I don't.
3 Do you eat crisps?   c Yes, he does.
4 Does your dog eat sweets?   d No, it doesn't.
5 Do cats drink milk?   e Yes, they do.
6 Do we run at school?   f No, she doesn't.

3 Write.

1  ____Do____ they go to school?   <u>Yes, they do.</u>

2 _____ he like the food?   _____

3  _____ it swim in the sea?   _____

4  _____ they work in a garden?   _____

4 Say it!

Do you watch TV?   Yes, I do.

eat

go

listen to

play

~~watch~~

Do you ...?	You	Your friend
(TV)	✔	✔
(tennis racket)		
(slide)		
(music notes)		
(tomatoes)		

12 Lesson 1

1 Read.

What do you do on Saturdays?

I play football.

What do/does ... do ...?

To ask what a person does *every day, every evening, every Saturday,* etc., we use the word **What** at the beginning of the question.

What do I/you/we/they **do ...?**
What does he/she/it **do ...?**

at the weekend
every day
on Mondays

Note: Use **on** before days of the week: *on Mondays, on Tuesdays,* etc. We use **at** before *the weekend.*

What do you **do** on Wednesdays?
I play football on Wednesdays.

What does your sister **do** at the weekend?
At the weekend, she goes to the playground.

What do you and your brother **do** every day?
We go to school every day.

2 Circle.

1 What **do** / **does** they do every day?

2 What do you **do** / **does** at school on Mondays?

3 What do **we** / **he** do after school?

4 **What** / **Where** does Marco do on Wednesdays?

5 What does your family do **on** / **at** the weekend?

6 What does your teacher do **every** / **on** day?

7 **Does** / **What does** your sister do on Sundays?

8 **What do** / **Does** your mum and dad do every day?

3 Write.

1 <u>What does Sue do</u> on Fridays?

Sue goes to the park.

2 _____ every day?

Mark watches TV.

3 _____ at the weekend?

I go to the cinema.

4 _____ on Sunday?

They do their homework.

5 _____ every day?

Lisa goes to school.

6 _____ every morning?

We drink milk.

4 Say it! **Write and say.**

What do you do on Tuesdays?

I play the piano.

Monday	Tuesday play the piano	Wednesday	Thursday
Friday	**Saturday**	**Sunday**	

1 Read.

When is your birthday party?

It's on Saturday!

Wh– question words

We use **Wh– question words** when we want more information than **yes** or **no** in the answer.

We use **What** to ask about things and actions.

What is this?
It's my bag.

What is Jessica doing?
She is swimming.

We use **When** to ask about time.

When is your English lesson?
On Monday.

We use **Where** to ask about a place.

Where is my book?
In your bedroom.

Where are your friends?
At the park.

We use **Who** to ask about people.

Who is he?
He's my brother, Tom.

2 Match.

1 Where are your shoes?   a It's a book.
2 Where is my schoolbag?   b We're playing a game.
3 What is that?   c It's on Monday.
4 Who is Tom?   d It's under the bed.
5 What are you doing?   e He's my brother.
6 When is the maths lesson?   f They're in the kitchen.

3 Circle.

1 A: **Who** / **When** is she?

B: She's my friend.

2 A: **What** / **Where** are they?

B: They're ants.

3 A: **Where** / **Who** is the cat?

B: It's in the garden.

4 A: **What** / **Who** is that?

B: That's the new teacher.

5 A: **When** / **What** are the holidays?

B: They're in summer.

6 A: **Where** / **What** is in your bag?

B: It's a toy cat.

7 A: **What** / **Where** is she doing?

B: She's sleeping.

8 A: **Who** / **Where** are the books?

B: They're on the desk.

4 Say it! Write and say.

What's your name?

My name is Michalis.

	You	Your friend
1 What's your name?	Alex	Michalis
2 Who is your best friend?		
3 What's your favourite animal?		
4 Where is your school?		
5 Where do you go on holiday?		
6 When is your birthday?		
7 What _____ ?		
8 Where _____ ?		
9 When _____ ?		

1 Read.

What time is it?

It's three o'clock.

What time is it?

To ask about the time of an activity, use **What time** or **When**.
What time **is it?**
It's twelve o'clock.

Use **at** with specific times (*five o'clock, midnight,* etc.). You can also answer
When-questions with a part of the day. Use **in** with *the morning, the afternoon*
and *the evening*. Use **at** with *night*.

What time do you eat dinner?
At seven o'clock.

What time is the party?
It's **at** six in the evening.

When do you do your homework?
In the afternoon.

When does your dad get up?
At six o'clock in the morning.

When do they eat lunch?
At midday.

2 Circle.

1 **What** / **When** time do you go to school?

   At / **In** eight o'clock.

2 **When** / **Where** do you have lunch?

   In the / **At** midday.

3 **When time** / **What time** is the party?

   It's / **Is** at five in the afternoon.

4 **When** / **What time** is the football match?

   It's in / **at** the morning.

5 I go to school **at** / **in** eight **at** / **in** the morning.

3 Write questions. Answer.

1 does / time / your sister / go to bed / What?

  What time does your sister go to bed?
  At five o'clock.

2 do / and dad / your mum / get up / When?

  _____

  _____

3 is / time / the / match / What / football?

  _____

  _____

4 to school / time / What / go / do / you?

  _____

  _____

5 it / time / What / is?

  _____

  _____

6 you / school / When / do / at / lunch / eat?

  _____

  _____

4 Say it!

at ... o'clock
in the afternoon
in the evening
in the morning
at midday
at night

When do you play football?

In the afternoon.

Review

1 **Write.**

1 Kim / play / football (✔)   _Kim plays football._

2 Tom / play / tennis (✘)   _____

3 He / fly / a plane (✔)   _____

4 Mum / watch / TV (✔)   _____

5 Karl / swim / in the river (✘)   _____

2 **Circle and answer about you.**

1 **Do /** (**Does**) your mum make cakes?   _Yes, she does. / No, she doesn't._

2 **Do / Does** you live in a city?   _____

3 **Do / Does** you like bananas?   _____

4 **Do / Does** your friends play football?   _____

5 **Do / Does** your dad drive a car?   _____

3 **Write questions and answers.**

| go to the library | listen to music | ~~play tennis~~ | play the piano | take photos |

your brother

1 _Does your brother play tennis?_

Yes, _____ _he does_ _____ .

you and your mum

2 _____

Yes, _____ .

your grandma

3 _____

No, _____ .

your cousins

4 _____

Yes, _____ .

your cousin

5 _____

No, _____ .

4 Write.

1 ? / do / they / what / do / in the evening
   <u>What do they do in the evening?</u>
   <u>They watch TV in the evening.</u>

2 ? / Nancy / does / play / on Monday / what
   _____
   _____

3 ? / do / what / they / do / at the weekend
   _____
   _____

4 ? / study / Brian / what / does / on Tuesday
   _____
   _____

5 ? / what / drink / Frankie / does / in the morning
   _____
   _____

6 ? / at night / Valerie / what / do / does
   _____
   _____

5 Write and match.

What	What	What time	What time	When	Where	~~Who~~	Who

1 <u>Who</u> is that girl?   a At seven o'clock.

2 _____ do you play basketball?   b It's seven o'clock.

3 _____ is a koala?   c She's my sister.

4 _____ do you get up?   d It's an animal.

5 _____ is my book?   e At the weekend.

6 _____ is it?   f It's on the table.

7 _____ are you doing?   g He's my uncle.

8 _____ is that man?   h I'm listening to music.

NATIONAL GEOGRAPHIC
L E A R N I N G

Wonderful World 1 **Grammar Book,**
Second Edition

Vice President, Editorial Director:
John McHugh
Executive Editors: Eugenia Corbo, Siân Mavor
Commissioning Editor: Kayleigh Buller
Head of Strategic Marketing EMEA ELT:
Charlotte Ellis
Product Marketing Executive:
Ellen Setterfield
Head of Production and Design: Celia Jones
Senior Content Project Manager:
Phillipa Davidson-Blake
Manufacturing Manager: Eyvett Davis
Cover Design: Lisa Trager
Interior Design and Composition:
Lumina Datamatics, Inc.

For product information and technology assistance, contact us at
Cengage Learning Customer & Sales Support, cengage.com/contact
For permission to use material from this text or product,
submit all requests online at **cengage.com/permissions**
Further permissions questions can be emailed to
permissionrequest@cengage.com

Grammar Book: Level 1
ISBN: 978-1-4737-6080-6

National Geographic Learning
Cheriton House, North Way
Andover, Hampshire, SP10 5BE
United Kingdom

National Geographic Learning, a Cengage Learning Company, has a mission to bring the world to the classroom and the classroom to life. With our English language programs, students learn about their world by experiencing it. Through our partnerships with National Geographic and TED Talks, they develop the language and skills they need to be successful global citizens and leaders.

Locate your local office at **international.cengage.com/region**

Visit National Geographic Learning online at **ngl.cengage.com/ELT**
Visit our corporate website at **www.cengage.com**

Photo Credits

10(ml) Artville; **10(mm)** Martin Ruegner/Radius Images; **10(bl)** Image Source; **10(bm)** Cheryl A. Meyer; **17(mr)** DigitalStock/Corbis; **23(4)** Karen Givens; **28(3)** Artville; **33(l)** NGL Reuse Library; **33(r)** Cathy Keifer; **47(2)** Studio 1One; **60(b)** Ingram Publishing/Superstock; **65(tm)** Gable Denims/500px; **65(br)** Nancy Brammer; **72(1)** BananaStock/Jupiterimages; **87(3)** DigitalStock/Corbis

© **Alamy: 14(2)** Blend Images; **27** Anna Stowe Travel; **38** D. Hurst; **47(6)** GlowImages; **56(ml)** Clare Charleson; **85(1)** Fancy ; **86(1)** Clare Charleson

© **Getty Images: 14(1), (4)** Alan D. Carey/PhotoDisc; **17(tr)** Creatas; **17(br)** Jose Luis Pelaez Inc/Blend Images; **23(3)** Arno Meintjes Wildlife; **28(5)** PhotoDisc; **47(4), 52, 55(bl), 59(b)** PhotoDisc; **59(d)** FatCamera/E+; **65(tl), (bl), 79(2)** PhotoDisc; **85(5)** Jose Luis Pelaez Inc/Blend Images; **87(6)** PhotoDisc

© **iStockphoto: 28(2)** Viorika; **28(9)** Midhat Becar; **37(6)** iStockphoto ; **55(mr)** Michael DeLeon; **62** Xyno ; **65(bm)** Kenneth C. Zirkel; **86(4)** Jophil

© **Shutterstock: 4** Szasz-Fabian Jozsef; **5(tl)** Andrey Pavlov; **5(ml)** Marinini; **5(bl)** Rena Schild; **5(tm)** Johan Swanepoel; **5(mm)** Dirk Ercken; **5(br)** Gemmy; **5(tr)** Ehrman Photographic; **9(t)** Wavebreakmedia; **9(b)** John Prescott; **10(t)** Chill Chillz; **10(mr)** Elena Schweitzer; **10(br)** Elena Odareeva; **12(t)** Graziano Vacca; **12(b)** Olga1818; **14(3)** Holbox; **14(5)** James Steidl; **16** Arbit; **17(tl)** Lotus_studio; **17(ml)** Gelpi; **17(bl)** Mistery; **18** Grigorita Ko; **19** Netkoff; **20** Ewais; **23(1)** D and D Photo Sudbury; **23(2)** Abxyz; **23(5)** Stana; **23** Yuyula; **24** Vadim Ovchinnikov; **25(t)** Macrovector; **28(t)** Butterfly Hunter; **28(1)** Andrey Pavlov; **28(4)** Ene; **28(6)** Nemeziya; **28(7)** Denis Rozhnovsky; **28(8)** 2happy; **28(10)** Nickolay Khoroshkov ; **32** Andrey Pavlov; **33(b)**; **34** Foxaon1987; **35(t)** Artisticco; **37** Foxaon1987; **37(1)** ChewHow; **37(3)** Ronald Sumners; **37(4)** Gelpi JM; **37(5)** Ely Solano; **37(7)** Nina Vaclavova; **37(8)** Antonio Gravante; **37(9)** Gresei; **39** Stockakia; **40(l)** Rafa Irusta; **40(r)** TerraceStudio; **43** Stockakia; **44** Sunny studio; **45(l)** Oleon17; **45(r)** Oleon17; **47(1)** Jacek Chabraszewski ; **47(3)** Tonis Valing; **47(5)** Kadroff ; **51(l)** Tony Moran; **51(r)** PhilipYb; **54** Z-art; **55(tl)** BlueRingMedia; **55(tr), (ml), (bl), (mr), (br)** Olga1818; **55(br)** Fotokostic; **59(a)** Eurobanks; **59(c)** Jacek Chabraszewski; **60(t)** Roger Clark ARPS; **61** Barmaleeva; **65(tr)** Konstantin Sutyagin; **65(ml)** Shutterstock; **65(mm)** Shutterstock ; **65(mr)** Juriah Mosin; **66** Zadiraka Evgenii; **68** Olga Guchek; **70(t)** Shutterstock; **70(m)** Aekikuis; **70** Shutterstock; **72(2)** Shutterstock ; **72(3)** Jack schiffer; **72(4)** Maria Dryfhout; **72(5)** WDG Photo; **72(6)** Bikeriderlondon; **74** Njjackson; **76** Picsfive; **79(1)** Gordana; **79(3)** Ivan Smuk; **79(4)** Olegganko; **79(5)** Markus MainkaShutterstock; **85(2)** Sandra Gligorijevic ; **85(3)** Ella1977; **85(4)** Monkey Business Images ; **85(6)** Greenland; **85(7)** Kirk Peart Professional Imaging; **85(8)** Alena Ozerova; **85(9)** Dusan Zidar; **86(2)** Eurobanks; **86(3)** Nenetus; **86(5)** Wavebreakmedia ; **87(1)** Levent Konuk; **87(2)** Piti Tan; **87(4)** Spaxiax; **87(5)** Larisa Lofitskaya

Printed in the United Kingdom by Ashford Colour Press Ltd
Print Number: 05   Print Year: 2023

MIX
Paper from responsible sources
FSC
www.fsc.org   FSC® C011748